Bright, Inhabited Lives

Ekphrastic Poems

Bright, Inhabited Lives

Ekphrastic Poems

by

Jenna K Funkhouser

© 2024 Jenna K Funkhouser. All rights reserved.
This material may not be reproduced in any form, published,
reprinted, recorded, performed, broadcast,
rewritten or redistributed without
the explicit permission of Jenna K Funkhouser.
All such actions are strictly prohibited by law.

Cover design by Shay Culligan
Cover image created on Canva
Author photo taken by Mary Gowan Photography
www.marygowenphotography.com

ISBN: 978-1-63980-564-8

Kelsay Books
502 South 1040 East, A-119
American Fork, Utah 84003
Kelsaybooks.com

Images are silent, but they speak in silence. They are a station on the way from silence to language. They stand on the frontier where silence and language face each other closer than anywhere else, but the tension between them is resolved by beauty.

—Max Picard

To all the bright, inhabited lives who have pointed the way.

Acknowledgments

My gratitude goes to the editors of the following journals, in which some poems in this manuscript first appeared.

Amethyst Review: "Leftover Miracles"

As It Ought to Be: "Persephone," "Chihuly's Baskets"

Ekphrastic Review: "Blind Girl Reading, by Ejnar Nielsen," "Like the Light, She Arrives," "Song of Love, by Nita Jawary," "Time-Molt, Tender, by Annaliese Jakimides," "Van Gogh Revisits His First Painting as a Ghost"

Geez Magazine: "Nighted," "Your Place of Resurrection"

Impspired: "Lake Swim"

NFSPS Honorable Mention: "The House of the World"

Oregon Poetry Association Anthology (First Prize): "Breathing"

St. Katherine Revies: "Hidden Life in Nazareth, by Ivanka Demchuk," "Doorways," "River"

A Time of Singing: "October Sap"

Vita Poetica: "Falling Star, by Romare Bearden"

Wee Sparrow Poetry Press: "Bark," "What You Love," "Ourselves in Rivers and Oceans," "Van Gogh Revisits His First Painting as a Ghost"

Contents

Breathing	13
Persephone	14
Chihuly's Baskets	15
Like the Light, She Arrives	16
Doorways	20
Falling Star, by Romare Bearden	22
Blind Girl Reading, by Ejnar Nielsen	23
October Sap	24
Hidden Life in Nazareth, by Ivanka Demchuk	25
River	27
Lake Swim	30
Your Place of Resurrection	31
Leftover Miracles	33
Nighted	36
Song of Love, by Nita Jawary	37
Bark	38
The House of the World	39
Van Gogh Revisits His First Painting as a Ghost	41
Red Dragonfly	42
Remembering Monet's *Coquelicots* in the Afternoon Light	43
The Heat of Summer	44
What You Love	45
Weaving	46
One Half	48
Mosaic Lessons	50
The Name of Things	51
Knowing	52
The House	53
What the Wind Was Speaking	55
Time-Molt, Tender, by Annaliese Jakimides	56

Breathing

I am trying, more than anything, to be
patient. No more dashing into the crush
of self-revelation. What do you want?
the silence is asking me, and I say
nothing, nothing yet. Standing at a bus
stop in the cold, simply breathing. The
sun waiting for me behind the blue haze.
It feels cliché asking the geese overhead
for inspiration, so I don't. I just watch.
Inhale. Unclench my hands.

Persephone

and what now / shall I write?

the trees armor against obsession / they are lucid / never
drink anything but the rain / and when the rain sings
to them / in their beds / they call it god /

oh when you came / in a hail of arrows
and leaves / and the wild deer / that night lightning
reversed / swallows went north / fig trees forgot
to worship / the sun /

there were a thousand Aprils / shouting your name.

Chihuly's Baskets

How carefully we preserve the emptiness
   in these theaters of light

how the man spins silken robes
   of turquoise and pebbled gold
     from the hot mouth of the kiln
and clothes oxygen in its fragile gowns,
    now
drawing its tensions away
   from the point where there must be
nothingness

                              cupped
in its pale, deep hands

and the prayer he breathes is nothing but
good, good.

To remain filled is
    to remain heavy

to resist your capacity to hold
invisible things
               to grow lucent
*lose everything
even your darkness*

let the fire touch you

it whispers

this bright shell husked
from the seed of eternity.

Like the Light, She Arrives

After Hammershoi

I.

Today you wake in a thick womb of silence, before it is pierced by your waiting life. You wake with one soft wing upon your mouth; a crease in your mind, an unspoken Thing, listening. Watch the morning now, sprouting its wheatfields of light upon the floor. Gather your thoughts within you like a fluted bowl, your skin breathing, particles suspended in air. Learn to grow heavy, palpable.

something in it thinks,
and is thinking without us
white bowls full of words

II.

A house with no memories is a chapel of moments, doors opening, windows with nothing to tell, and breath, the pale green seeping out of the walls, reminding one how kindred they are, lung and mind, necessary as air. The table stands beside her, emptied into the now, attention settling like dust. The mirrors silent on the walls. Soon, we become the standing, mind paused with expectation, body alert like a silent watcher of birds, convinced that any moment we will walk through . . .

you shout, and she turns
her head; you have chosen the
memory, she says

III.

What does she stand for, placed like an object among objects, obscured from us, hinted to us? Like the light, she arrives without explanation, a presence which neither needs nor shuns you, and all gains meaning in association. She waits for no one to return, no one to blame, holding the keys there in her darkened hands. The room is solid with her shrouded form, blessing us eternally from the wooden chair, which will never die. Bound within time, we project our faces onto hers, invent stories, miracles. The heavy truth of her silence will outlast them all.

through the glass, a soft
suggestion of first snow, a
sea with no waves, tide

IV.

To become the light, first you must sit in darkness. To become a fount, first the dark field, swallowing rain. Light is a knowledge that follows itself through darkness, wise of its own existence, placid joy unassailed, stark carrier of common grace. All things trust as it spreads its body beneath their feet: take this free gift of myself, and with it, grow. When you find that still, porous space within you, it is ready to climb in.

she waits, with her tray
of desire, outlives us
the solitude blooms

V.

I have to believe a room is placed like this, bruise-purpled, cotton swabbed, swimming in its own muffled light. Precarious moment, tending towards the sentimental and the symphony, suggestion of crayon, small knitted caps. Particles clump through the curtain like timid droves of bees. And she, dark as midnight, absorbing and absolving all

from the soft altar
she kneels, half-assenting fact
in the pastel dawn

VI.

How many faces a room wears; how many faces we bring within its doors. The day is beginning, the day is ending, night and encore of night, always the frame. This moment, immortalized—this one man's window, nobody's mirror. Does a true thought exist before it arrives, paperweight in the palm of the mind, meant for weighing down the infinite? Paint lies thick on the flesh, canvas. Three bricks of light crash through the window, anchor into the hazy blue.

who is behind the
lens: the seeing one? The moon
climbs the wall. Waves break.

VII.

Mystery is the silver mouse I suggest to you in the corner. Again you turn to remember, this needle between the cracks, thread of sheer muscle and the waking doubtfulness of ghosts. Now the walls are slate, weighted and ancient, burying their shadows beneath a succession of doors. She has disappeared from this poem.

swirl of fingerprints
like molded clay across
the surface. *is. was.*

Doorways

Wind ripples off
   the shaggy tops
of mesquite trees
   and threads a ribbon
of bending grass. The ground
   is stern and red like brick
except for the man-made trail
   of gravel snaking
into the horizon.

There is a doorway
   in everything. This
is what the man
   who was nearly my grandfather
was saying
   in so many words.

Men had lived here,
   generations scraping
a life off the hard, red soil;
   hope threaded through death
in weddings and hayings
   and the soft ears of new
calves every spring.

There was a name
   for everything and the hot earth
carried its ghosts and stories
   like the hidden wells we searched
for under the blue grass.

It was a baptism of the mind,
   a clothing of your eyes in the names
and histories which became the keys
   to unlock the doors.

Then were the layers of story
   stacked among the slow,
craggy mountains
   and the wild plains

and the world became a cup
   into which generations had poured
the unadulterated meaning
   of their lives.

The cracked blue jug
   on the porch steps
and the old barn
   and the larkspur planted
by grandmothers past

are not happenstance, any more
   than the crickets that sing
you to sleep in the summer nights.

They exist as part
   of a speaking whole,
fragments of a story
   we can choose to exit,
but can never be untold.

Falling Star, by Romare Bearden

She is the only one left
in the world

and the left arm, unhurried,
wise in the way
it anticipates the miracle

body split down the line
of ordinary and catastrophe
one basket filled with living
and two small cups
waiting to be filled
   (with joy? with sorrow? with delight?)

while our minds wear the same circles
                        over and over
into the tall, wild grass

to which
does she lift her china cup
in recognition

to which
does she salute
as she stands there,
outwaiting the mirror,
outwaiting the sun?

Blind Girl Reading, by Ejnar Nielsen

Incidental to the evidence
   That meaning proves
Like a dough,

That thoughts do reach out
        From the page
And claim us, knead
           Us into form, rise

—An experience of the word
So bodily, eyes
        In the meeting
Of print and finger,
        Each word
A journey your hand
Must travel, send postage

Until the very shape
          Becomes an object
           In itself:

Here the delicate curve
         Of a question
The scalding exclamation

Here the wood ferns
         Batting their damp eyelashes
         Against her legs,

The scent of a small happiness
And the relentless sound of rain.

October Sap

The trees are a little in love
With dying, flushed
With October sap as it
Stirrups through their veins.

They know nothing
Of how we philosophize
On what they offer us
How we talk so much
On death, while they
Offer us wide platters
Of resined light.

In the sharp breath
Of the morning
A thumb-print sparrow
Couches the green pear
Of its body
Against the leaves

Watches
All day long
As the electric men
Heap up death
In perfect little piles
Of sunlight.

And green, green, says the bird.

Hidden Life in Nazareth, by Ivanka Demchuk

An east wind,
   she might have thought
as she splayed
   the wooden beams
and divided their
   garments

Brushed aside
   the hammer and nails
one more time
   to lay down that quilt
of many colors.

Then: the tenderness
   of a father's stance,
poised in readiness behind
      a tottering boy—

an eagerness
   in her body kneels,
welcomes

this young skin-weaver and his
weak steps, brazen
arms flung in eager trust

     her eyes
ever on his blossoming,
sun calling him outward
      into Light.

In time, he will eclipse
her own becoming; in time,

she will watch his winds blow
where they will, sourcing from
that unseen fire.

But here, this moment
   frozen and burning
with a pure and holy joy:

for one long and wild breath,
   it is only
this current of delight,
   this miracle of a gift
given over again

each so eager to be given,
   so eager to adore;
this silent, ordinary trinity.

River

I.

a bird which is not quite
a heron rests by the slow river
and the ripples caused
by little eddies around its gray
spinster feet trickle down
the water's sleeve
out of sight.

i thought, then
of the way the rivers
wind like a damp mythology
through every mind—
the way they stand, always,
for more than themselves.

while the herons
and the birds which are
not quite herons

stand looking
for something, maybe
only fish

a river runs mad
through a man's mind.

II.

perhaps
there is a mythology
in this:

when wheat fields bend
we call them a river

and the wind is the river

and the river is always
running through your mind.

wild, wild, the bird sings.

III.

what is it
that a river means—
or perhaps, what does
it not mean—

which is everything
that is still and stagnant
everything lost
to change

because the river speaks
and its every word
is a dance of movement
unrepeatable
and eternal.

IV.

and so, perhaps,
the river is the most
immortal creature
on this mortal earth

eternally recreating
its own life.

V.

here we stand
on the bank of its
eddied waters
and watch the herons
baptize themselves
for flight

hungry for such openings
to draw us out, something
to spend the life-force
rushing up inside

else all of it
is lost

even
as we try to protect
it, the algae grows.

Lake Swim

Like satin sheets, one could feel
the sun-dappled lake receive you

a weighty gift, gliding in and out
of its tucked-back corners

fresh and cool and alive

and you are indistinguishable,
fused into movement

you exert yourself for the pure joy
of reaching, your breath heavying

your heart singing into your brain.

You could stay weightless
forever, if only the shoes
(so practical for a summer's hike)
did not recall you to ground . . .

Your Place of Resurrection

I.

The indigo windowpane
Of a tulip's stained-glass heart—
Strangeness and pleasure,
Mystery of interior sight.

Here, the underside
Of a brash crow's wing.

Here a ray of light
From the depth
Of shipwrecked bones.

II.

Life is designed
To be seen through.

The ancient Celts believed
In spiritual wandering
Until you found the place
Of your resurrection.

But nowhere do they tell you
What you are looking for
      Why you find it in moments
        Of strange, aching, ridiculously
          Mortal things—
Like the ribbed porcelain of a violet seashell,
Even more beautiful
Knowing some small thing
Shaped it from their own desire:

While they lived, the moonrise mural inside
Known only to their own
Intimate satisfaction.

III.

Close your eyes in the thin winter light.
Let the tumult burn within you
—all desire and fear, all fighting spirit
of flesh and fretfulness.

You do not need to be always seeking resolution,
wrestling down peace.

You do not need a theory
Just a way of life-birthing
into this wildly possible world.

Let the questions roar in their swirling winds,
their salty foam, their stinging fire.

Seek the wildness
as your place of resurrection
And let it make you
Alive.

Leftover Miracles

For Calais

My mouth is narrow.
I cannot open it wide enough
to feast on all that a day offers.

Example: today
the sky is a sinkhole
writing in watercolor
which the crows are circling
(those slicked, stern critics)

there are eleven new roses
swathed around sticks
like tufts of pink cotton
almost too sweet

and a man stops
to tug a bit
on his daughter's jacket
and answer why
for the seventh time

he nearly misses
the shuffling bus
on which everyone notices
each other
and pretends not to

on which two women
will tell him, *what a sweet
child,* and he will glance
at another man's newspaper
surreptitiously.

Onion skins waft
their way into everything

a promise of tomorrow's
bounty, and the handprints
climbing up the walls
like a prayer.

And one mother holds
a sick child close
to her breast, incarnate
Madonna of the one
resting in the corner.

The waves
never stop breaking.

Anything
could be
ahead—

tiny fingers
iridescent with suds
wild mornings
that suddenly grow still
the steel blade of hope
knifing its way through
a kind of despair

it is too much
to chew;
I am gulping
the world down whole
I am managing
only the crumbs
the leftover miracles
piled into baskets

(nothing is wasted
after all, keep the
big meals for the ones
with larger stomachs)

I am watching the world
break open and multiply
before my very eyes.

Nighted

A flourish of golden poppies
Shouts my name, and I walk along
The road of anger a while
Before I stop and listen.
Here there are two pavements:
On one side, the sin of doubt,
On the other, the sin of being sure.

I wait here for the moon to rise
And gather the burning poppies
In its softer hands. I wait
For the silent, knowing strokes
Of the darkness to blend the two lines
Like a painter into something true.

This is a waiting to welcome
The slight negligence of the
Light-less, the way it shadows
Everything into sisterhood;
The yes of the bright poppies
And the nighted road.

This is placing your hands
Into the dark wounds of God.

And this is because
A man once told me,
A wound is a crack in the armor;
A slit in a fence. It's the only way
The wild and living things
Get through.

Song of Love, by Nita Jawary

Think of Delft tile,
Shipwrecked and smashed
By ocean breakers,
Washed ashore in fragments
Of placid ladies, windmill spokes,
Tulip petals and hunting parties.

All those silent factories, painting
An ordered life upon the smooth cream
Of kiln-fired certainty.

And all this chaos, jumbling life
Into the reality of love
And loss
And irreplaceability.

Bark

What you cannot see is our insistence. We strain not to clasp but to mirror, to frame, to exert a boundary line amidst the void of the infinite. To become self is to become surface: layers and layers of nearly nothing, added over time into existence. We are grasping for self, for reality; mottled, skin like a tree bark, chrysalis—always the outer fragility, the inner strength. Does anything else ache with such gorgeous loneliness?

The infinite laps
at our existence. We molt.
We ooze out, alive.

The House of the World

Now dusk
drops its sheer
curtains
over the bruised hills

Now the door
of the day's light
closes
with a crimson
shudder, leaves
the porch light
stuttering on
for the moon.

Hogs and leopards
return to her
dark hearth;
flowers genuflect
and softly enter
their dim cathedrals.

And the restless ones
stir a hidden fire
on the other side
of the wall.

A cat at the window.
The chaos
of scattered wings.

The house is
gently turning
its face away.

The porch light,
out.

The click
of the lock.

Van Gogh Revisits His First Painting as a Ghost

I've seen this street hundreds
of times, sometimes
even in my dreams.

So what is it about one man,
slouching down the canal,
the light like dawn,
the way the lines
are stone and water
skeleton and key?

Fog makes us intimate,
shapeless, he and I
just a handful of neighborhood
undistracted by a wide expanse
    of sky.

When the curtains part halfway
like a careless mouth
we flow like water
into their open lives.

Red Dragonfly

While I am thinking
   How best to frame him—
The pungent light, the lotus stalk
   The gauzy tips of his lucent wings

He goes, graceful
   And impatient as calligraphy
A thing of fire and crepe
   Sprung from the fury of molten stone

Leaves me imageless
   And burning.

I had not known I needed it—
   His utter freedom, after so long
Of damp and wooden seasons

But he became for me
   Both the hot breath of summer
And its absolution

A startling spike of joy
   Fleeting
And immortal, both

A gift that blesses me
Beyond itself

And lusciously eludes my grasp.

Remembering Monet's *Coquelicots* in the Afternoon Light

Perhaps she stands in your memory
The way I first saw her—a woman
Determined to be alone with her thoughts
The day, warm and languid
And she, miles from tea shops
And town gossip, wills the day to lengthen
Allows her son to romp far
Into the wild red fields.

The sun is a coin of gold
Slipping into her bare hands.

For a moment, something like happiness
Startles her, a bird sputtering
From its nest, disappearing
Into the thin blue wish of a sky.

The Heat of Summer

The lawn is full of clover
And beetles slick and opaled
As oil spills. The moth-eaten
Wheat fields are turning gold
And coughing up their dust.

We move slowly, resent hurry
And effort, find ourselves drowning
In the blue
       blue
          blue of an endless sky.

The world is so harsh and fabulous.
The clover enfolds me.
   The fields eat me alive.

What You Love

After an untitled work by Adrian Pitts

About life, even if you don't know it,
   Are the questions.
Where are we all going, and why?

Sometimes the brilliance blinds everything,
You say to me. *We glide a world coated*
   Like a sheet of ice
Until one of us happens to splash through.

Look around:
Everywhere, there are the thin,
Brave spaces: jagged doorways
To whatever lies beneath.

And the horizon, you say, *becomes the yes*
That can't hold out the opening.

We are carrying this, we are carrying each other.
All of us are walking into the light.

Weaving

The cloth is stronger for the waiting
for the layered tensions
and the turns and circle-backs
combed close along the taut,
slender lines.

They say that weaving
first began
not for clothing
but for shelter

supple reeds and birchbark
rendered lasting by the careful
meaning-making of a pattern—

thus the wind has fewer
holes to whistle through.

In this apartment building
I am rubbing warp lines
with my neighbors.
Parallel and nestled close
the slender skein of lives
unravels in a dance of

under, over
each trailing a little world
of its own normality

the scents of biryani
    and fish sauce
mingling at dinner hour

wild bicycle rides
through the courtyard
dance parties, barking dogs

ingredients of a life
worn durable by the choice
to stay; to keep one's thread
as part of the woven whole

all our knotted loops,
our backward lines
rendered into something
stronger,
         something
to stay the bitter cold.

One Half

With what fervor we tore
the earth apart that day,
gleefully uncovering spade
after spade of fallow clay
scented of rain and loam,
exclaiming after each appearance
of writhing earthworms
like hermits airlifted from their
silent caves.

You leaned on a shovel
under skies that threatened,
but did not rain, and watched
me scatter seeds like we
may never see another spring.

How many packets of zinnias
and forget-me-nots did we fling
to the wind and whims of a garden?
And for all that, this evening I count
only seven leggy sprouts
peering back at me.

The mathematics of gardens,
like us, my love, remains a mystery.
In the end, was it all for the brief flush
of a flower? Or could it also have been
the sweat, the crumbling virgin earth,
the muddy thrills?

You could say
so many things have to die
for only seven gangly beauties
to be born.

Or you could say
that after all,
we tore the earth open
to each other, inhaled her
secret breath like the language
our bodies speak without us

caressed the all the dark places
and their secret kingdoms
rhizomes and roots needing
no reason but their own life-hunger.

You could say
the part above ground
is only one half
of a wild and hungry world.

Mosaic Lessons

The play of light is the first and last rule of mosaic.
—Terry Tempest Williams

The mender of light
places stone
    into softness
learns what the glass
tells her of its desires
   fragments of frozen river
light arrested into place
and form.

Allow the breaking, she says.
   Shatter yourself open.
   Always find the dissonance
and make it sing.

Braiding light,
like a quilt of emptied stars,

she trusts some night to scour away
   the layers of grit and darkness
   (necessary in their blunt sturdiness)

trace the glowing pattern of her life
with a calloused palm
eager and unafraid.

The Name of Things

Sitting here in the green thumb
of my neighborhood, I listen
to the confession of strangers,
neighbors who curse over phones
and earbuds, seeking
some kind of absolution.

Words are like that.
They walk out of your mouth
like a line of ants
foraging understanding.
Given a crumb,
they'll keep returning.

    Finch, Sparrow, Kinglet.

This spring, the tall grasses
are full of songbirds.
Camus and black nettle
thrive on the wild edges
of this block, a planned wilderness
over an industrial waste site.
The man beside me is learning birds,

wants to know the name
of things. Still, words
keep flitting into this space,

keen, hungry, rustling
for crumbs in the undergrowth.

    Thrush, Warbler, Nuthatch.

Every year, they return to the nests
we thought had been abandoned,
sing through all the doors we meant,
in our winters, to keep closed.

Knowing

Often, as the jutted trail garnished
with late-November leaves
disappeared under our feet,
   we turned back
     to recognize how far we'd come.

In the narrow, moss-smothered canyon
we'd been held in sound
as if a womb: entire

our past and present absorbed
into the ocean
   thundering over rock cliff
   and deafening our lives.

Now we work our way back through the trail
before sundown, choosing the higher path
with its crumbling bridge, our ears
still roaring with an echo
of that primal world,
   feeling all the way home
   we had lost something

trusting that at some
inconsequential moment of mindlessness
this light hitting the last golden tree at dusk
will be given back to us

as we turned, then, for that final glance

knowing, somehow, the way your body trusts
to find the lip of the cup in the dark.

The House

I.

This is the part of the story I always leave out:

you, making breakfast in front of the stove,
the radio on, both of us longing
for a hundred conflicting things.

I'd like to talk
about all the ways
we've ripened over
ten years, the way
we've been drawn
into a fuller
creation of ourselves.

So much has been delicious.
Yet all ripe fruit softens,
brown spots appear.
The bud has to begin again.
The fragile fruit grows slowly,
slowly on the vine.

II.

Becoming real means
becoming faces
as an icon takes shape

layers and layers of nearly nothing
repeated
until flesh and self and image
reveal themselves
upon a surface of pure light.

Even the childless conceive
a third life, that which exists
through and beyond them
nourished by the exact
joining of their lives.

In a decade we have built little
but these hidden layers

old selves imperceptibly tinted
by each thing we have loved
and lost; our selves the best
measure, if not of flawlessness,
then of grace.

We walk home in the twilight,
in this city we have chosen, and
I can see the outline of your profile
by the fading light.

In spite of ourselves
                        our life
is the house we've built together.

What the Wind Was Speaking

For L

it came in the April clouds
like a fury
rode its horses
with their bridles cold as steel.

it spoke in the words
of the space between
two syllables

a haiku of emptiness
a hand still curved just
after the moment
of being clasped.

do you remember, sister,
what they said
the wind was speaking?

they said:
not all open mouths
are empty ones.

to have loved
  at all
is never loss.

Time-Molt, Tender, by Annaliese Jakimides

It's all there:
The dusk, the wind
The monarchs
And the autumn leaves

The bicycle you crashed,
And the wire fence

Petals of sunflowers
Cactus, carpet,
Grass that arrived home
On a picnic blanket
Honeycomb and hot asphalt

Black seed of illness, grief
Pressed between the thin
Rice paper of your chrysalis

This oldest metaphor
For powerlessness,
    Risk

When Time becomes merely
The snakeskin of your eternity

What thrills
Is this most human pain:
No choice
Over the color
Of your next wings.

About the Author

Jenna K Funkhouser is a Pacific Northwest native who has been delighted to experience places of awe and community around the world. Some of her greatest heroes are Celtic mystics and Dostoyevsky lovers. When she isn't nose-deep into a mosaic or letterpress project, she seeks language as a space to embrace and stay awake to the dualities and mysteries of daily human existence.

You can find her and recent works at:
jennakfunkhouser.com

www.ingramcontent.com/pod-product-compliance
Lightning Source LLC
Chambersburg PA
CBHW030915170426
43193CB00009BA/863